My Big Dinosaur Book

Triassic Dinosaurs

These dinosaurs lived between 252 and 201 million years ago

Eoraptor was one of the earliest dinosaurs. This tiny creature may have had hollow bones much like modern day birds.

Munc

Riojasaurus was one of the largest herbivorous dinosaurs of its time. It had a long neck and tail.

Herrerasaurus had a long, narrow skull and was between 3 and 6 metres (10–20 feet) long.

Plateosaurus had a long, mobile neck and teeth that were leaf-shaped.

Coelophysis was a small, yet deadly, predator with a long, pointed head and sharp teeth.

Mussaurus means 'mouse lizard'. The smallest dinosaur egg ever discovered was that of a *Mussaurus*. It was only 2.5cm (1 inch) across.

Whoosh!

Peteinosaurus was a tiny flying reptile with a wing span of only 60cm (23 inches). It ate insects and had a long tail.

Plateosaurus

Plateosaurus was one of the earliest plant-eating dinosaurs. It was very common in Europe and lived in the late Triassic period.

Like many plant-eating dinosaurs, *Plateosaurus* probably also ate small stones to help grind up food in its stomach.

A long tail helped *Plateosaurus* to balance.

Plateosaurus was about 8 metres long (26 feet) and weighed about 700kg (1543 pounds).

Plateosaurus had a small head and little sharp teeth.

on its large back legs to reach tall plants.

Plateosaurus probably spent some of the time standing

Plateosaurus had five fingers on each hand, three of which had claws.

Jurassic Dinosaurs

These dinosaurs lived between 201 and 145 million years ago

Even though it only ate plants, *Heterodontosaurus* had three different types of teeth for biting, tearing and grinding food. It was the size of a turkey.

Brachiosaurus was a huge dinosaur, measuring 26 metres (85 feet). Unlike most other dinosaurs, its front legs were longer than its back legs.

Allosaurus was a fierce meat-eating dinosaur and has been called the 'great-great grandfather' of *T. rex*.

Megalosaurus walked on two powerful legs, had a short strong neck, arms with three fingers and sharp claws.

Archaeopteryx also lived in the Jurassic period. It is one of the oldest known birds and was about the size of a magpie.

Crack!

Diplodocus was a large herbivore. Its very long neck measured up to 8 metres (26 feet) and its whip-like tail could stretch to 14 metres (45 feet).

Stegosaurus had thick, strong legs, giant plates along its back and four big spikes on its tail.

Megalosaurus

Megalosaurus was one of the first dinosaurs to be discovered and named. It was found in England in 1676 and named in 1824.

Megalosaurus had a bulky body, short neck and heavy bones.

Megalosaurus means 'big lizard' and it measured 9 metres (29 feet). It was discovered before scientists realised that even bigger dinosaurs had existed!

Sharp claws on each of its fingers and toes helped *Megalosaurus* grab its prey and pin it down.

Because it had a huge head and a large brain, *Megalosaurus* would probably have been very intelligent.

Megalosaurus was a fierce hunter and meat eater, with a large, powerful jaw and sharp teeth.

Megalosaurus carried its heavy weight around on two strong legs.

Stegosaurus

Stegosaurus was a plant-eating dinosaur with short, chunky legs and a double row of bony plates along its back.

Stegosaurus had a very small brain. It was only the size of a walnut!

At the end of its pointed skull, *Stegosaurus* had a toothless beak.

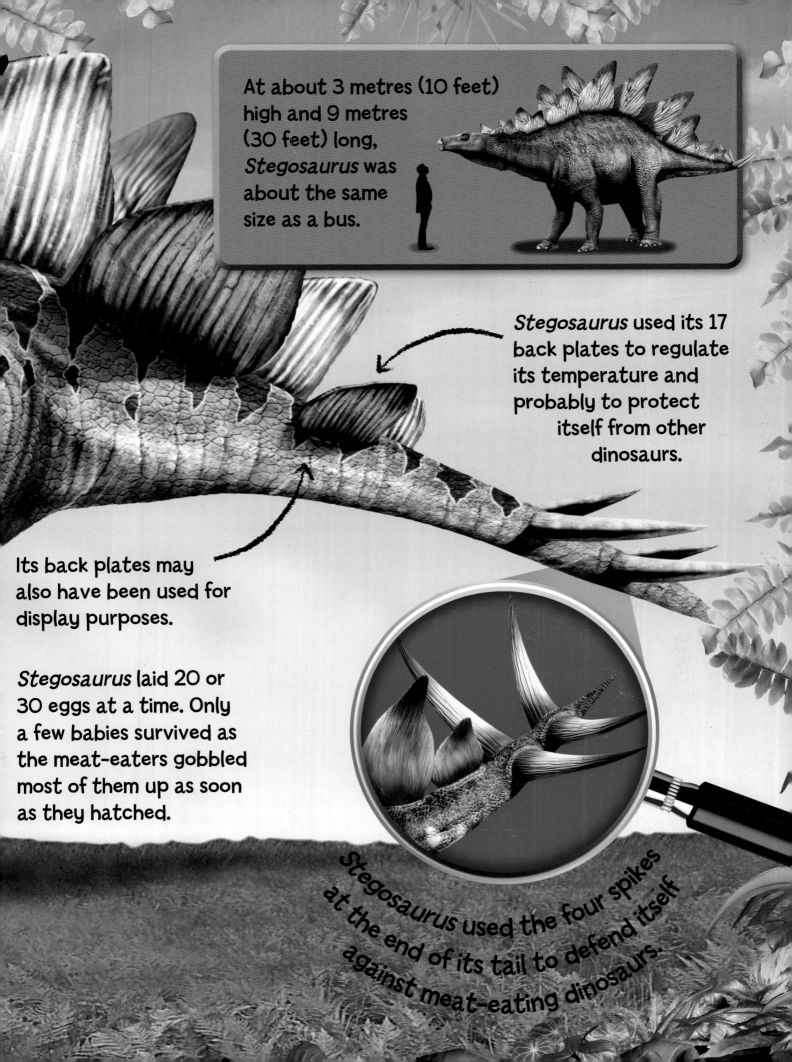

At about 3 metres (10 feet) high and 9 metres (30 feet) long, *Stegosaurus* was about the same size as a bus.

Stegosaurus used its 17 back plates to regulate its temperature and probably to protect itself from other dinosaurs.

Its back plates may also have been used for display purposes.

Stegosaurus laid 20 or 30 eggs at a time. Only a few babies survived as the meat-eaters gobbled most of them up as soon as they hatched.

Stegosaurus used the four spikes at the end of its tail to defend itself against meat-eating dinosaurs.

Diplodocus

Diplodocus was one of the longest creatures ever to walk on Earth. It lived in areas of western North America towards the end of the Jurassic period.

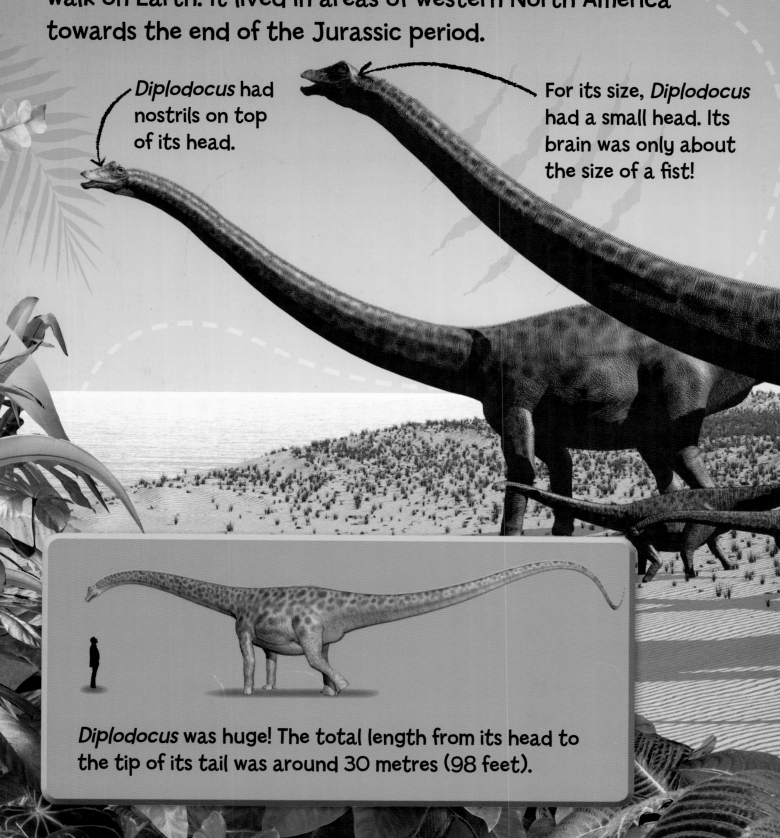

Diplodocus had nostrils on top of its head.

For its size, *Diplodocus* had a small head. Its brain was only about the size of a fist!

Diplodocus was huge! The total length from its head to the tip of its tail was around 30 metres (98 feet).

To frighten other dinosaurs away, *Diplodocus* made a cracking sound with its whip-like tail.

Diplodocus was a plant-eating dinosaur. It used its peg-like teeth to grind up tough leaves.

The back legs of *Diplodocus* were longer than its front legs.

Some scientists think that *Diplodocus* might have 'dropped' its eggs while walking.

Cretaceous Dinosaurs

These dinosaurs lived between 145 and 66 million years ago

Triceratops had an enormous skull, a protective neck frill and three large horns on its head.

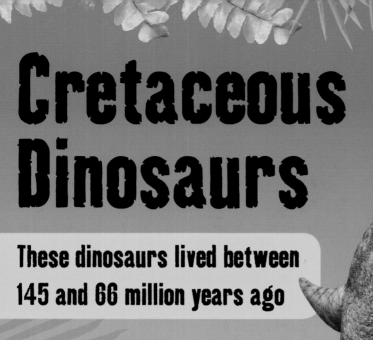

snap!

Velociraptor means 'speedy thief'. It was roughly the size of a turkey, but could run at approximately 40mph.

Kronosaurus was a large, ferocious sea reptile that also lived in the Cretaceous period. It swam in the seas that covered parts of Australia.

Elasmosaurus was a sea reptile that lived alongside the dinosaurs. Its very long neck was over half the length of its entire body and had 75-76 bones!

Ankylosaurus had bony oval plates and two rows of spikes on its back, as well as a huge club-like tail.

Roar!

Tyrannosaurus had two powerful legs, two tiny arms and lots of sharp, pointed teeth.

Pteranodon was a flying reptile. Its wingspan, which measured up to 10 metres (33 feet), was greater than any known bird.

Tyrannosaurus rex

Probably one of the most famous dinosaurs, *Tyrannosaurus rex* (*T. rex*) was one of the most fierce and deadly.

T. rex had a huge skull with a strong jaw over 1 metre (3 feet) long.

Its huge saw-edged teeth would crush the bones of its prey.

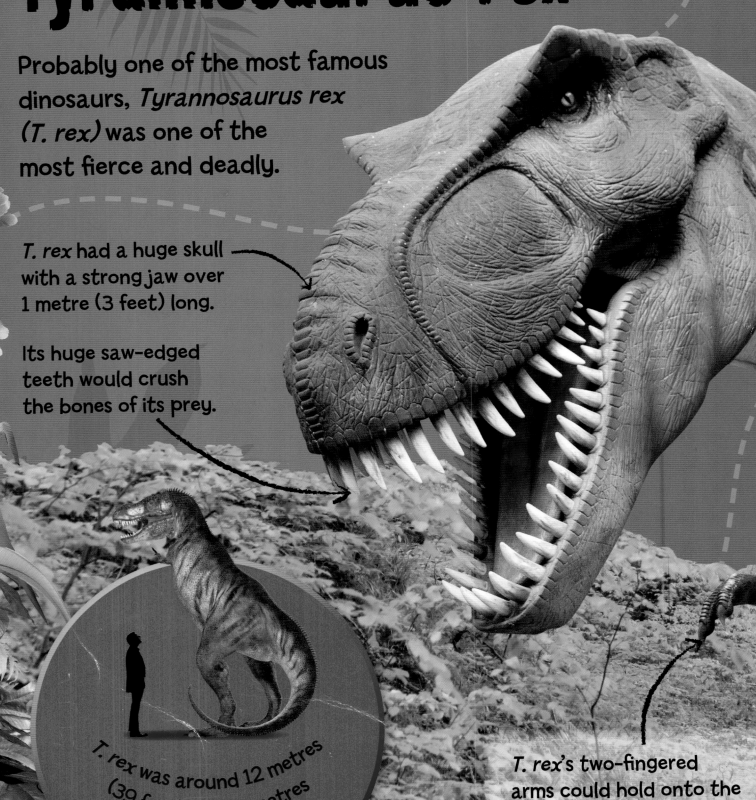

T. rex was around 12 metres (39 feet) long, 4 metres (13 feet) tall and weighed about 7 tons.

T. rex's two-fingered arms could hold onto the prey, but they were too short to reach its mouth.

Scientists believe that *T. rex* could eat up to 230kg (500 pounds) of meat in just one bite.

Powerful thigh muscles and a long tail helped *T. rex* move quickly.

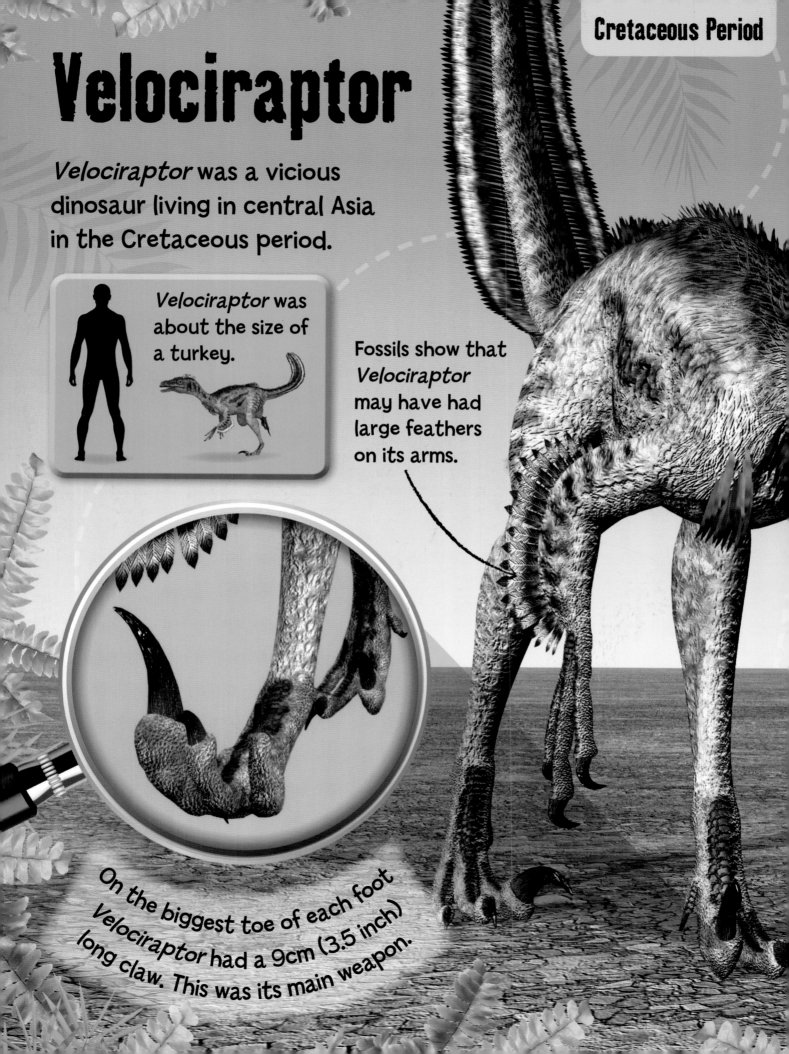

Velociraptor

Velociraptor was a vicious dinosaur living in central Asia in the Cretaceous period.

Velociraptor was about the size of a turkey.

Fossils show that *Velociraptor* may have had large feathers on its arms.

On the biggest toe of each foot *Velociraptor* had a 9cm (3.5 inch) long claw. This was its main weapon.

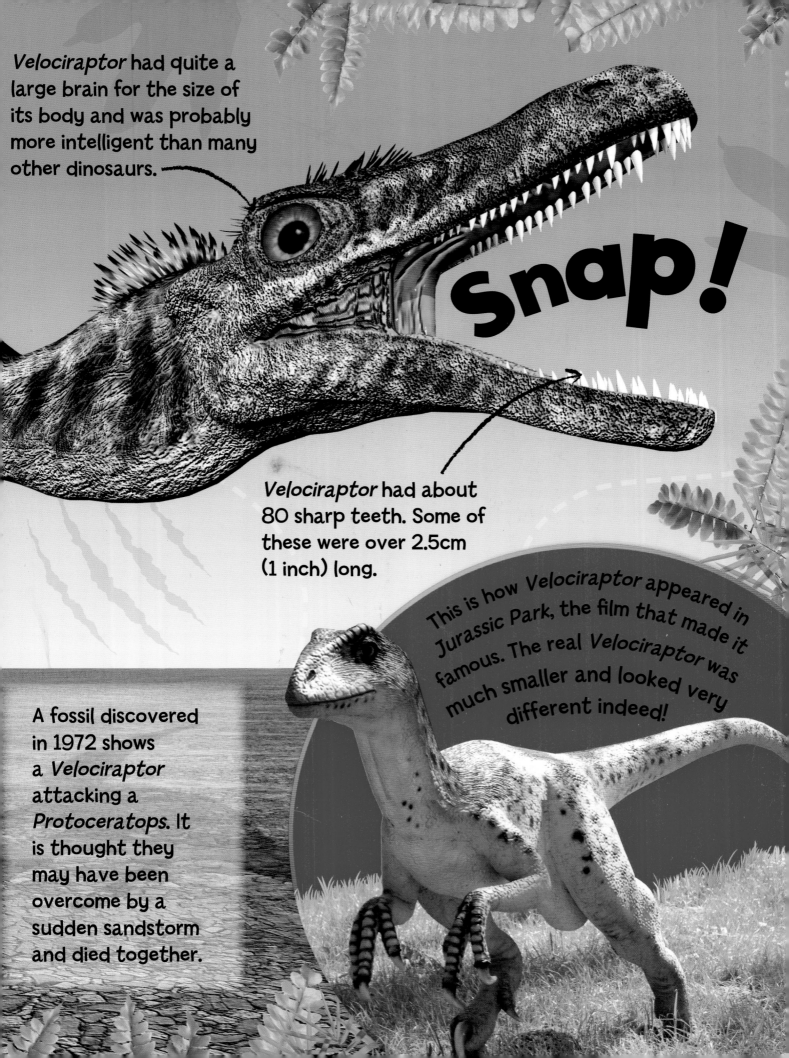

Velociraptor had quite a large brain for the size of its body and was probably more intelligent than many other dinosaurs.

Velociraptor had about 80 sharp teeth. Some of these were over 2.5cm (1 inch) long.

Snap!

This is how *Velociraptor* appeared in Jurassic Park, the film that made it famous. The real *Velociraptor* was much smaller and looked very different indeed!

A fossil discovered in 1972 shows a *Velociraptor* attacking a *Protoceratops*. It is thought they may have been overcome by a sudden sandstorm and died together.

Triceratops

Even though *Triceratops* looked fierce, it only ate plants. It lived at the same time as *T. rex*, in western North America.

Triceratops' bony frill protected its neck and probably helped to keep it cool, too.

Triceratops used the three horns on its head to defend itself against meat-eating dinosaurs. The two longer horns could reach 1 metre (3 feet).

Triceratops had a parrot-shaped beak and powerful jaws for chewing plants.

Meat-eater *T. rex* had an appetite for *Triceratops*. We know this because bits of *Triceratops* bones have been found in fossilized *T. rex* dung.